Dad's Laws
for
Happy Living

Daniel Edwards

WESTGATE
PRESS

Spokane, Washington

Published by Westgate Press, N. 5901 Lidgerwood #117, Spokane, Washington 99207.

Library of Congress Catalog Card Number: 96-90271

ISBN   0-9652449-0-3

Dedicated to your mother,
the most wonderful person in the world.

Dad's Laws
for
Happy Living

Dear Children,

Before you leave our home to start homes of your own, I want to leave you a little written collection of some of the things your mother and I have tried to teach you while you were growing up. I suppose parents have always tried to pass on some advice and tell their children the "right way" to live. I decided to put this advice in book form – a sort of summary of what we think will help you to live happy lives.

Sometimes we get so busy in our daily lives that we get bogged down in the everyday hustle and bustle and lose track of the "big picture." In today's world, many people have lost sight of their overall goals, and are struggling along toward secondary goals which lead them down blind alleys.

Every now and then, we get a little glimpse of the big picture. Not too long ago, during a Christmas vacation, all you children were home with Mom and me; everyone was healthy and in good spirits. I recall one evening in particular when your mother was in the kitchen with all five of you. I was sitting in the family room doing some paperwork, and when I finished, I turned around in my chair and looked over toward all of you. Mom was wearing her apron and hurrying to get the turkey out of the oven. The rest of you were stirring the vegetables on the stove, icing the cinnamon rolls, and filling glasses with ice water. Delicious aromas drifted through the house and a wonderful spirit of cooperation and peace filled the kitchen. You were all laughing, singing, and talking happily together. All was well with the world.

I'll never forget what happened then; it was one of those rare moments when the petty worries of daily life are swept away and we are allowed to view the entire picture of what life has to offer us. I got a brief glimpse of celestial joy – pure happiness unadulterated by the usual mortal concerns. I saw clearly that true happiness is not found in the worldly accomplishments or fame so sought after today, but in the warmth of family associations.

This is not a new or novel idea, but is one of those things that each person must discover for himself. It is not a great mystery once you have seen the big picture. The mystery is that much of the world today has neither learned nor passed this on to subsequent generations.

Our greatest wish for you is that you live happy lives, and Mom and I will ever work toward that end. I hope that this little book of "laws" will help.

Love,
Dad

Introduction

Living happily ... there are probably as many ideas and philosophies about how to live happily as there are people who are actually trying to be happy. Everyone must discover for themselves what it is that constitutes happiness; the problem is that many people figure it out too late to do anything about it. Mom and I don't want that to happen to you, and have been trying throughout your lives to point you in the right direction.

I believe there are some principles in life, which if followed, will help you avoid many of the problems which lead to unhappiness. I have called these principles "laws," and have listed twelve of them. The first nine concern our dealings with ourselves, with God, and with other people. And because we live in a world where material concerns can lead to so much unhappiness, I have added three laws concerning personal finances. Some are pretty basic, and others are quite far-reaching; some of the laws encompass many concepts, others just a few. When there are many concepts within a law, I have included what I call a "corollary," or smaller law. The laws and corollaries will be easily identifiable, and hopefully will be easy to remember.

None of these laws or corollaries are really new ideas, none are written in stone, and there are exceptions to every rule. But your mother and I think that most everything in here is pretty good advice. I know you'll recognize most of these ideas from your growing-up years, and I hope this little book will help you pursue a lifestyle which allows you to be truly happy.

That man who lives for self alone
Lives for the meanest mortal known.

Cincinnatus Hiner Miller

The First Law

In the 1300's, a disease called the Bubonic Plague swept across Europe. It had happened before, and would happen again, but this time it was so destructive that it was referred to as the Black Plague. The disease was devastating. One fourth of the population of Europe was wiped out; whole villages were destroyed. Families were decimated; women were widowed, children were orphaned. The whole fabric of the society was left in ruins.

The manifestations of the disease itself were terrible, with fevers, chills, swollen and draining glands, sepsis, pneumonia and death. The vectors or carriers of the disease were fleas which lived on rats; and in the Middle Ages, the rats were everywhere. Although the fleas lived on the rats, they were willing to live on and bite humans, too. The actual causative agent of the disease was a bacterium endemic to rats and carried by fleas.

In those days, medicine was primitive, and the treatments for the plague were as varied as they were ineffective. Incantations, chants and spells were all used to no avail. The rats multiplied and the disease swept through the land leaving destruction in its wake.

Today there is a new plague in the land. It has also swept through civilization before and will undoubtedly do so again. Today, however, we are witnessing an epidemic unequaled in magnitude. The effects of this plague are not dissimilar to those of the Black Plague. There is great destruction in the family, divorce, abandoned children, crime, violence, poverty, substance abuse, and an overall loss of morality.

The carriers of this disease are as ubiquitous as the rats in the Middle Ages. They are magazines, books, television, radio, movies, and even some of the people with whom we associate every day. They carry the agent of this disease into our homes and into our hearts ... infecting us.

The agent of today's plague is not a bacterium; it is a character trait. The agent is *selfishness*.

Governments are fighting this moral plague just as ineffectively as the Black Plague was fought. Enormous sums of money are spent on police departments and public health offices, mental health counseling and school programs, day care and welfare programs. But the plague worsens and spreads. Today's therapies are no more effective than the spells cast in the Middle Ages against the Black Plague; like the rats in the Middle Ages, today's carriers multiply without restriction.

The preoccupation with self has had a long history and some persuasive apologists, but not until recently has it become so pervasive. Beginning in the 1960's, our society began to emphasize the gratification of self over everything else. Physical pleasures, contempt for authority, and the shunning of responsibility were themes which began to be trumpeted. As the years have rolled on, the influence has become more widespread; and as we have become more sophisticated, the doctrine of self-ism has become more acceptable – even desirable. Our aged are abandoned in old folks homes, our children are left in day care centers, mothers choose the workplace over the home to find fulfillment, and men abandon their responsibilities as husbands and fathers. Moral decay runs rampant.

The cure for today's plague will not be found in government expenditures or in community programs. It is a personal and individual dedication to look outside of one's self which will halt the spread of this moral plague. A population of selfless individuals will form a nucleus for a society free of the ailments of today's disease.

Each of the other laws in this little book, especially those dealing with our relationships with others, are dependent on our being unselfish. Selfishness is the major cause of the breakup of marriages and families. It is the primary ingredient in financial failure. It is the underlying cause of moral decay.

There are several things we can do to avoid selfishness. First, we must recognize those influences which emphasize our own gratification over selfless motives. Such influences are everywhere and in many instances have become the norm for our society; be observant, for many of these influences are very attractively packaged. Second, we can choose a lifestyle and a specific pattern of behavior that will aim us in the direction of unselfishness. We must consciously decide to live a life with other people in mind. Third, we must evaluate our motives in everything we do. We will come to understand that happiness is found when we are thinking of others.

Every day of your life you will interact with others, and face the pressure exerted on you by all the influences of the world. Beware the plague of selfishness.

Law Number One

Shun Selfishness

Set all things in their own peculiar place,
and know that order is the greatest grace.

John Dryden

The Second Law

Throughout our lives there are forces pulling us in one direction or another. Work and friends and family – perhaps awards and recognition, money, maybe even fame. All these things can influence us and our attitudes. In today's world we can observe external pressures influencing the choices people make, and subsequently, the direction their lives will take.

Your mother and I once attended a week-long professional education meeting. On the last day, we sat in on the "personal living" section of the meeting. One of the men spoke about his own life. He had worked terribly hard and was world famous in his field. Despite this fame and the accompanying wealth, he said, "If I had it to do all over again, I would spend a lot less time at work, and a lot more time at home. My marriage ended in divorce, and my children are strangers to me."

It was evident to everyone in attendance that this man felt he had misplaced the priorities in his life. We each have to establish a list of priorities for our own life. Everyone has his or her own list, whether it is written down or not. Many people who are highly successful in business or sports or entertainment have made the pursuit of that success such a high priority that most of the other aspects of their life have suffered. It is essential that you sit down and make a list of priorities for your life. Do it now, while you're old enough to make good observations and while you're young enough to be idealistic.

As an example, I'm going to give you a list of the priorities that Mom and I have established and are trying to live by:

First, be good people – honest, forthright, hardworking children of God. In every aspect of our lives we should try to emulate His example.

Second, be a good husband or wife. It is the most important relationship we will have with another human being, and will govern our entire life.

Third, be good parents. Our success in life will depend largely on how we do as parents. Our children and grandchildren are a pretty good measure of our contribution to the world.

Fourth, be good providers or homemakers. Despite what you will hear or read today, providing for the temporal needs of the family is the responsibility of the husband.

The men of the world are the principal providers for their families. Perhaps even more important is the necessity for women to be good homemakers. They must make the home a refuge from the world – a place where love can grow and children can flourish.

Fifth, contribute time, energy, and resources to the church, and help others in the church.

Sixth, participate at schools and in the community, and involve ourselves in hobbies and other worthwhile activities.

These are *our* priorities in their order of importance to us, and we think they are good ones. But you must establish your own list of life priorities, and *live* that list. It doesn't do any good to say your family is more important than your work, then spend all your time at the office while your family suffers. The world is filled with people who have declared one set of priorities and are living a different set; they can't figure out what went wrong when things don't go the way they envisioned.

How do you live the priorities you have set? There are some built-in safeguards. If you have decided that living a good life as a child of God is the most important thing you do, then acting like a son or daughter of God will follow. If being a good spouse is of great importance, your concern for the feelings and welfare of your spouse will direct you to keep that a high priority in your life – your spouse will be your most important partner in life's decisions.

Together you and your husband or wife can make policies which will govern your actions and help you remember your priorities. For example, Mom and I decided that both of us would not leave you children at home with a babysitter to go and do church work. (You were always our most important church work.) We have also tried not to leave home more than one night on any weekend.

You must periodically review the policies you've set and insure that you're "sticking to your guns." Early in your life, you'll face major decisions concerning the priorities you have established. Once you have made those decisions, it is easier to make the same decision the next time it comes up. Pressures in life can cause you to shift your emphasis, and this shift can occur gradually, so review your priorities with your spouse and make sure you're not getting off track.

It is easy to get bogged down in the the everyday trials and tribulations of life. Short-term changes in priorities can offer immediate solutions to some of these difficulties, but long-term problems are often the result. You must keep the big picture in view, and don't miss seeing the forest when you're in the middle of the trees.

Set your life priorities carefully, review them frequently, and stick to them.

Law Number Two

Prioritize your life, and live your priorities

Choose you this day whom you will serve…
but as for me and my house, we will serve the Lord.

Joshua 24 :15

The Third Law

Tapestry making is one of the loveliest forms of art. A tapestry is made by weaving colorful horizontal threads, called the "weft," around a series of vertical threads which are attached to a loom. These vertical threads are called the "warp." When completed, only the horizontal threads are visible, though the vertical threads have provided the foundation on which the entire tapestry is woven. The finished product is, in essence, a woven painting – beautiful to behold.

Each person's life is like a tapestry; our thoughts and deeds, our goals and aspirations, our husband or wife and our children, our friends, our work and our play – each is part of the weft, the series of threads which we have woven together to form something lovely and unique – the tapestry of our life. Our gifts and our talents, and what we do with them, add beauty and color to the design when it is completed.

The warp of our life's tapestry remains unseen, but gives the structure and support to the tapestry and holds it together; without the warp our tapestry could never have been begun nor enlarged. God is the "warp" in the tapestry of our lives. Without Him we have nothing, do nothing , and are nothing. All things are His and all we have is given to us by Him. Every part of our lives – our education, our talents, our spouses, our children, our professions – everything is built upon the foundation granted to us by our Father in Heaven. And everything we do in life should be done with that in mind. We cannot and should not try to divorce God from anything we do in life.

"Wait a minute !" you say. What about yard work, what about homework, what about the ten thousand other things we do in everyday life?   We do all these things within the context of our relationship with God, and we must remember that.

We are of divine heritage. A child of God has unlimited potential and capabilities, but is dependent on God for all the blessings in his or her life. God loves his children unconditionally, and yet asks them to do their best – even to become like Him. In everything we do, in every daily task, we must remember our heritage and act accordingly.

If we think about how grand and expansive the creations of God are, it helps us to keep ourselves, our abilities, our talents and our accomplishments in perspective. All we possess, all we are, all we do, and all we can become is by virtue of the grace of God; we are always reliant on Him.

He asks that we worship Him, and that is only as it should be. But what does it mean to worship God?

The worship of God involves including Him in every aspect of our lives. We cannot abandon Him while playing basketball or golf, while on vacation, or at the office. In addition to keeping Him in our minds and hearts, we are asked to communicate with Him in prayer, to read the scriptures, and to actively live the gospel.

We need to dedicate to God what is His: our time, our talents, our resources – everything we have. In the Book of Matthew we are commanded to, "... love the Lord with all our heart ... soul ... and mind."

We must be involved in the church. We can serve God and man best by being actively committed to working in the church. Just as a hot coal removed from the fire soon cools, so do we lose our closeness to our Father in Heaven if we remove ourselves from the association of the church. Go to church; be involved.

Remember to be children of God twenty-four hours a day, seven days a week. Obey the commandments. Give thanks in all you do, serve your fellow man, and be charitable. In your tapestry, weave a lovely series of threads onto the "warp" that is our God, and never forget that He is our Foundation.

Law Number Three

Worship God

The first and best victory is to conquer self.

Plato

The Fourth Law

There is one person who is responsible for each of your decisions – every thought and every deed. Everything you think, say, or do is the responsibility of … you !

No one else can make you think, say, or do anything you don't agree to. It is each person's responsibility to be the master of the self – and there are many areas in which control must be exercised.

The first great area to be considered is one's mental outlook on life. You've probably heard about the two frogs who were out for a "hop" around the farm when they accidentally hopped into a bucket of buttermilk. They could not reach the bottom of the bucket, and were forced to swim to stay afloat. Soon they both tired. One of the frogs, realizing they were not going to be able to last much longer, said to his companion, "It's hopeless. I can't go on." He quit swimming, sank to the bottom of the bucket, and drowned. The other frog said to himself, "I'll never give up !" and despite his fatigue, swam even harder. He paddled the bucket of buttermilk into a lather. Before too long it began to harden, and soon the entire bucket was filled with butter. He caught his breath, hopped out of the bucket, and went on his way.

So it is with us. If we can keep a positive mental attitude, we can accomplish anything. Even in the face of terrible odds, we must look at the bright side. Look at the glass as half full, rather than half empty.

Corollary

See the glass half full

Be objective in your thinking. Remember that everyone has ups and downs; it's human nature. If you can think objectively you can overcome low times and stay under control during high times.

Control your thoughts and avoid letting your mind wander into unwanted places. We are given a great gift at birth; we can only think about one thing at a time. We can walk, chew gum, and bounce a ball at the same time, but we can only *think* about one thing at any given time. This endows us with great power to control our thoughts. Fearful, depressing, or depraved thoughts might slip in, but can be overcome by replacing them with uplifting thoughts or the words of a song or poem. It allows us to guard against evil or unworthy thoughts, depressing or counter-productive thoughts, even boring and unimaginative thoughts.

Corollary

Think Good Thoughts

Another area to be addressed is that of our emotions. Emotions are a great gift which allow us to feel life's joys and sorrows. We experience happiness, sadness, fear, love, and hate; the whole range of human emotion. As mentioned above, we all have emotional peaks and valleys and we must be prepared to deal with these ups and downs. Anger and other negative emotions can be especially destructive if allowed to go unchecked. We can exercise control over anger by avoiding those things which anger us, preparing ourselves to control our responses, and even by altering our outlook to such an extent that those inciting stimuli no longer anger us. Emotions are wonderful things, but don't allow your emotions to run, or run over, your life.

Spiritually, we can be the master of ourselves as in every other way. We are often led to believe that we must sit back and wait for spirituality to descend on us like the dew. Nothing could be further from the truth. As individuals, we can consciously seek to live a better life, to communicate with God more earnestly, to read the scriptures more, and to donate our time and resources to the church and to other people. As families we can pray and read together, serve others together, and actively worship together. These individual and family efforts will result in an outpouring of blessings from heaven. By our own efforts, we can realize the blessings of heaven in our lives. Just as we can exercise control over our thoughts and emotions, we can control the spiritual side of our lives.

We must also exercise control over our physical bodies. We have to control our intake of food and not eat improperly or excessively. (Or diet excessively, either !) We also need to avoid those substances which decrease our ability to control ourselves or are addictive. We must allow ourselves an appropriate amount of rest and exercise.

We can control our thoughts, our

emotions, our spirituality, and our physical bodies, and develop habits which will allow us to be masters of the self.

Along with governing ourselves, it is essential that we continually try to *improve* ourselves. The story is told of Pablo Casals, the great cellist, who continued practicing and performing in his old age. Someone asked why, after all those decades of work, did he continue his daily practice regimen. It is said that he smiled and replied, "Because I think I'm getting better."

We ought to always try to improve our minds, as well as our physical skills. We must expand our knowledge and horizons and develop the talents which have been given us. We should become appreciative of as well as participants in the arts, both visual and auditory. We can improve our skills in writing, music, artwork, and other creative endeavors, and should continue to educate ourselves – not only in the area of our professions, but in all areas. Study and learn – expand your horizons. Stay abreast of what's happening in the world.

We must also stay in good physical condition and improve our physical skills. It's not a bad idea to pursue a physical skill which you can develop over time and continually improve throughout your life.

Set goals and write them down. You can still learn to play the piano – even at an advanced age. Grandma Moses didn't start painting until she was seventy-six years old !

If you can discipline yourself and improve yourself, you will like yourself. You are of Heavenly Parentage and have unlimited potential. Live so you can like yourself. If you don't like something about your nature – change it ! Be flexible. Be adaptable. Make yourself a better person !

Law Number Four

Master Yourself

God sells us all things at the price of labor.

Leonardo da Vinci

The Fifth Law

There are a few principles in life which will never change. One of these defines us as creatures of industry, develops the traits of goal-setting and perseverance, and gives rise to creativity and invention. It provides us with a living, gives us opportunity to serve others, and allows us the satisfaction of accomplishment. It is not only essential for our livelihood, it is essential for our self-worth, and is one of life's great blessings. The principle is that of work.

There are all types of work , and nearly all of them are worthwhile. Although your work with your family is the most important of all your labors, it is still necessary to obtain a living outside the home. You can choose any number of careers, but you should choose carefully. Most often, the career you choose will be your career for your entire life. Learn your aptitudes and skills. You may like working directly with people, or you may prefer working at a computer terminal. You might enjoy working with your hands, or you may like to restrict your work to thinking. Almost all honest work is good and worthwhile; you just need to work at something that is fulfilling and that will allow you to be self-sufficient.

There are some general principles that will help you with your work, and they apply to all kinds of tasks.

Work Hard.   Half-hearted efforts lead to half-baked results. We must apply consistent, concentrated and diligent effort to our tasks, or we will not be successful.   This applies to studying math, writing a business plan, grading a building site, or doing heart surgery. Even the most menial of tasks can be accomplished more readily if we apply concentrated effort.

It is essential that we do quality work. I learned this lesson early in life. One of my jobs as a youngster was to mow the lawn. We had a push mower that cut the grass fairly closely. My Dad insisted that the grass be cut in one direction, then cross-cut again in the opposite direction.   One hot summer day, I had just finished the second cutting when my Dad came out of the house, looked at the lawn and said, "Cut it again."   Admittedly, I had not done excellent work, and he was not impressed. After I cut it the third time, he came out of the house, looked at the lawn and said, "Cut it again." So, I did. When I was done, he told me that the lawn looked great – and it did. In fact, it had never looked better than it did that day. Quality work will always stand you in good stead. Remember that every profession has its moments of boredom and tedious, repetitive work. Medicine, law, motherhood, education, banking – each profession has its element of tedium. It's all part of any job and has to be dealt with. Work, whether in the home, or outside the home, demands application of all the characteristics of self-discipline discussed in the last chapter. Your work may require ingenuity, diligence, even occasional inspiration; mostly, however, it will require perseverance. Set goals and work diligently to meet them.

Work fast. Everyone has seen people who are barely moving while they labor at a less than desirable job. Work can be done quickly or slowly. Each person has several speeds at which he or she can work, and each task has an optimal speed at which it can be performed. Working at an excessive rate can be detrimental, causing us to make mistakes or tire before the task is done; but insufficient speed leads to boredom and loss of concentration, lengthens the time required to accomplish the task, and puts us behind in our work. When you begin a job, decide what the optimal rate of work will be, and stick to it;

not too fast to do quality work, and not so slow as to waste time. There are many benefits to working quickly. Time is saved; time that can be used to do other things. Working quickly requires sustained concentration, which usually yields high quality work. And if the task is an unpleasant one, you get the added bonus of being done with it sooner. You must be cautious not to overdo; mental or physical exhaustion is a real danger. Take breaks when you need them – exercise moderation.

Corollary

If you're getting behind in your work ... work faster.

Work efficiently. There are many different ways to complete a task and do it well, and there are some guidelines you may wish to follow. Organize your work and approach it in an orderly fashion. I remember shoveling snow with my big brothers. I was quite little at the time, and rushed out to help them in their labors. I began making haphazard inroads in the snow on the driveway when they told me to watch the pattern they were using to remove the snow systematically. It was my first introduction to actually planning a task and following the plan. Not only was it much faster and more efficient than my random shoveling, it was *easier*. Often, the best method is also the easiest – and still yields high quality work. In addition to organizing, the most efficient way to accomplish work is to stay on task. If you allow yourself to be distracted, you lose continuity and your work suffers.

Now that I've said all this about work, let me mention not working. James Howell said, "All work and no play makes Jack a dull boy," and that is true. Rest and relaxation are important to recharge our batteries. You should plan to rest, plan for vacations, and maintain balance in your life. But get your work done first; it's a lot easier to rest when there is nothing hanging over your head.

Corollary

Work First, Play Later

Work is a great gift we have been given. It is not to be avoided or given short shrift, but to be treasured as a blessing.

Law Number Five

Work Hard, Work Fast, Work Smart

In character, in manners, in style, in all things,
the supreme excellence is simplicity.

Henry Wadsworth Longfellow

The Sixth Law

Sooner or later, we all have to decide on what kind of life we want to lead. I don't mean what kind of work we do, or what socioeconomic level we will aspire to. What I mean is what sort of person do we want to become. How will we affect those around us? Will we be treated as a friend? Will we be loved by our family? Will we like ourselves? These are important questions and will be key points in deciding our ultimate worth.

We should want to do our best in every aspect of our lives – in educating and improving ourselves, establishing and raising a family, serving other people, developing a career, and in seeking financial security. Regardless of how successful we are in each of these areas, it is essential that we avoid elitism.

I know an older man who is quite wealthy, having made a fortune in land development and construction. The unusual thing about him is that he is almost universally loved and respected. Why? Because he never considered himself one bit better than anyone else. When workers were needed at the church orchard, he was there in his overalls pruning trees with everyone else. When he was asked to teach a children's class, he did so willingly.

We are all children of God, equal in His eyes, and equally loved by Him. Be careful not to place yourself above others for any reason. There is a great temptation among the well-educated, the socially conscious, the spiritually-aware, and particularly the economically well-to-do, to think themselves superior to the rest of the world, and to try to impress others with their self-declared status. Don't do it ; it is a mistake, and ultimately leads to alienation and unhappiness.

Corollary

Avoid Elitism

There are some ideas which can help you to choose a simple and unassuming lifestyle. Avoid consciously trying to impress others in everything you do. If you are financially successful, remain moderate in your possessions. Buy a moderate home, (a nice home, even very nice, but moderate) and a moderate automobile. Even if you can afford to buy a mansion and a Rolls Royce, I can't think of any good reason to do so. You can live very comfortably and have nice things without being ostentatious. The same holds true for your educational achievements or artistic talents. Share your knowledge and your gifts in such a way as to uplift and help others rather than to astound your friends.

Choose quality friends from all walks of life. There are ways to associate with those of a different socioeconomic status than yourself. Send your children to schools where they will meet all kinds of people and be involved in the school's activities. Give community service. Attend and be involved in church. Good people and good friends are to be found everywhere.

Do physical labor. Work around the house and work in the yard. Even if you can afford to hire someone to do all the menial tasks around the house and yard, do what you can yourself. Dig in the dirt – get dirt under your fingernails; it washes out. Mow the lawn, plant bushes, grow a garden. Hard physical labor, especially working close to the earth, helps us keep ourselves in perspective; we should not be above doing all types of work.

Corollary

Dig in the Dirt

All these ideas are calculated to help keep us from thinking that we're more important than the next guy ... because we're not ! A person can be well educated, talented, culturally enlightened, and financially well off, but is not superior to anyone else. Be willing to laugh at yourself and be careful to avoid haughtiness or false sophistication. Do your best, strive for the best, but live simply.

Law Number Six

Choose Simplicity

Neither is the man without the woman,
neither the woman without the man, in the Lord.

1 Corinthians 11:11

The Seventh Law

Iron is one of the most widely used metals in the world. It is strong and durable, but is dark and dull in appearance, and is subject to rust and corrosion. Chromium, on the other hand, is a hard but brittle metal which cracks and fractures easily; yet it is highly resistant to rust and corrosion. When polished, it is brilliant and shining. Because of their weaknesses, neither of these metals alone can be used to make many of the products we utilize in industry, hospitals, or our homes. However, when iron and chromium are purified, refined, heated, and combined together, they form an alloy – a strong, resilient, and beautifully shiny metal which is resistant to rust and corrosion. This alloy is stainless steel, which is used to make knives, kitchen utensils, pots and pans, and thousands of other useful items.

People are not unlike iron and chromium. Some are very strong, but are subject to the corrosive effects of their surroundings. Others are bright and shiny, but are brittle and have difficulty withstanding life's pressures.

When two people properly and thoroughly go through the refining process of dating, courtship, and marriage, it is not unlike the combining of two lesser metals into a strong, attractive alloy. They become a single brilliant unit, resistant to corrosion and wear, resilient against external forces, durable and everlasting.

Early in life, we begin the purifying process by trying to become the person we would like to be, but at some time we must make decisions about marriage. These are the most crucial decisions of our entire lives. When? Where? Who? Entire books have been written on the subject, and I don't intend to try to do that, but a few ideas about marrying well and staying married are probably in order.

How do you decide who you would like to marry? It is an active process involving a conscious effort and lots of thought. The first thing you have to do is figure out what *type* of person you want to marry. This is a pretty involved process in itself, as there are a lot of different types of people. You'll probably be better off with someone a lot like ... you ! If you choose to marry someone with an educational background and work ethic similar to yours, you will have a lot better chance of being happy. Try to find someone with similar goals, and similar likes and dislikes – even someone who is fairly similar to you and your family in appearance. There are some successful marriages where none of the above similarities exist, but not many. You will probably want to choose someone who comes from a good family, a family like yours. You always hear, "You don't just marry the person, you marry their family, too." There is a lot of truth to that. But more importantly, your future spouse will be a lot like the family he or she came from. The men will treat their wives and children a lot like their fathers treated their mothers and them. And the women will treat their husbands and children a lot like their mothers treated their fathers and them. Seek out individuals from families which are like yours; families where the parents are in love with each other and involved with the children. If your future mate's family has similar religious, economic and educational goals, you will be much better off.

How in the world are you going to find someone like that, with a family like that? Well, you don't find jewels in a rock pile, and you won't find the kind of husband or wife you're looking for in a tavern, either. Watch other people; watch families. Watch your parents and the parents of your friends, and observe how they treat each other. Frequent places where families gather, and where children of good families congregate. Go to church. Attend good colleges. Frequent good places – that's where the good people are !

Once you are in those kinds of places, you have to date a lot of different people, and lots of different types of people. You must be somewhat aggressive – dating is an active process which requires a lot of effort. You have to take some risks. We all have fragile egos and no one likes to be rejected, but you can't sit back and wait for life to come to you.

Corollary

Take Some Risks in Dating

Dating! How? When? Why? Relationships with the opposite sex start in childhood, but they are not always congenial at first. I remember when one of you boys was in the third grade, and I asked you if you knew a little girl in your class – her mother had told me that you and her daughter were classmates.

"No," you replied.

"What do you mean, 'no'? She's in your class, how could you not know her ?" I asked.

You looked at me quite matter-of-factly and said, "I don't keep track of *them* !"

Later on, however, you do begin to "keep track of them," and at age sixteen or so, you can start dating. Begin dating when you are sixteen, and go on group dates. The idea is to learn to talk with and have fun with members of the opposite sex, to learn to enjoy each other's company – not to pair off immediately. Watch the people you associate with and you will see different patterns emerging. Some people will be attractive to you and others will not; some will be exciting, and others will be boring. It is a great adventure getting to know lots of people and learning who and what you like.

Eventually you will begin dating one-on-one, when you are mature enough to want to, and mature enough to enjoy being alone with someone of the opposite sex. It is even more important to be observant when you are going out on individual dates. You should have fun and enjoy yourself, but in the back of your mind, be observant.

Every   relationship   has   a   level   of

commitment associated with it. People who have just met and are anticipating going out on a first date have absolutely no commitment to each other. But after a series of dates, you may find yourself attracted to one individual with whom you would like to spend a lot more time. Your commitment level rises. If you decide to date the same person exclusively, your commitment level rises again. At each stage you make a conscious decision to increase your devotion to each other. (At each stage, it also becomes more difficult to undo your commitment.) Eventually a couple decides that marriage is right for them, and once again they increase their commitment level.

All this represents a natural progression starting with that first uncomfortable association with the opposite sex and ending with the ultimate commitment to marry each other. There are some caveats you should apply to the entire process.

Don't start dating too young; don't date individually too young; don't marry too young ! How young is too young? I don't know; but I can tell you that the majority of the divorces I have seen have occurred in marriages which began when the couple was too immature to be objective about their feelings and about their future spouse – too immature to analyze their goals, and to make good judgments. Rather than saying, "Don't marry too young," I should probably say, "Don't marry before the right time."

Corollary

Don't Marry Before it's Time

On the other side of the coin are those people who are waiting for that perfect spouse to come along. The Flawless Individual. The White Knight. The Cinderella Princess. Well... they don't exist, and if you decide to wait for him or her to ride into your life, you're in for a long wait ! Whatever ideal person you have conjured up in your imagination is unlikely to come knocking on the door. Remember that the person you marry won't have a lifetime of experience behind him or her; your spouse will be young and inexperienced– just like you! Look for character traits which they have and which you think they will probably develop: honesty, integrity, hard work, ambition, tenderness, and patience; the same traits you are trying to develop yourself. Look for someone who loves the Lord. Remember that your white knight or your princess may only be a squire or lady-in-waiting when you meet.

Corollary

White Knights Develop over Time

You'll probably notice I haven't mentioned love. A whole library of books has been written on love. You will fall in love and marry the person you love. Just remember that love is a delicate thing. The love you have for your intended spouse is like a seed that is carefully planted and cultivated. While this love is a seedling and is becoming a young tree, it requires intense cultivation and protection. As it grows, the attention needed is not lessened. Even when your love is mature and becomes a mighty oak, unshakeable in even the fiercest storms, it still demands constant care. Relish your love, enjoy your love, but constantly nourish it.

Corollary

Nourish Your Love

When you have made the decision to marry … marry forever ! Don't plan to fail. Plan right from the start to stay married forever! These days, a lot of people get married with the idea that if it doesn't work out just the way they want, they can just get divorced. No problem. With a plan and commitment level like that, they are sure to fail. Choose your mate wisely and never even consider divorce; plan for the eternities. It's a greater commitment than "until we don't get along," or "until the kids are gone," or even "until death do us part." When you commit to each other forever, your day to day care for each other will reflect that commitment.

The way you treat each other will spell success or failure, happiness or misery. Treat each other like a king or queen; each day show your spouse that you love him or her. Don't be rigid about chores around the house. Men can change diapers, do dishes, and run the vacuum as well as their wives, and women can pick weeds and plant flowers as well as their husbands. Recognize each others' needs, and meet them.

Greet each other lovingly every day. Mom and I have a tradition that whenever I come in the door after work, I drop what I'm carrying, and Mom drops whatever she's doing, and she runs across the room and jumps into my arms. It may seem silly, but it is an important expression of love and devotion as well as a form of communication. It says, "You're more important than anything else."

Corollary

Greet Each Other Lovingly

Communicate ! You must talk to each other, and listen to each other. Take the time to really listen to what the other has to say. Sometimes it will require more effort than at other times, but it is an absolute necessity. Call each other now and then, let your spouse know you love him or her. Pray together each day.

Plan to encounter problems in your married life, and plan to resolve them. Compromise, discuss, and plan – work each difficulty through until you have solved it. Many different types of problems will arise. Children: how to discipline them, how to educate them, how to reward them, how to deal with their problems; you may have differences of opinions on how to deal with these and other issues in childrearing. Money can also be a problem, to say the least. Money usually creates difficulty if you don't have enough, or if you have too much, or if you have just the right amount. Mom and I have found that we can't just discuss money on the spur of the moment; if we do, we tend to disagree vehemently. So we have devised a system. When one of us feels the need to discuss family finances, we go to the other person and say, "We need to have a budget discussion." This alerts the other that a delicate conference is required. We schedule a meeting, prepare in advance, and open the discussion with prayer; and we do just fine. It sounds like a lot of trouble, but it works !

One or the other of you may develop health problems, you might lose your job, or you might have problems with extended family. Lots of things can cause trouble; plan in advance to discuss them, and overcome them.

Remember that you met each other and fell in love when you were dating. Don't stop. Date your entire life, every week. Even if it's not an expensive date – just a walk in a park and an ice cream cone; go out once a week without the children. Make memories which will last forever. Play together. Plan activities that you both enjoy so you can do them together all your lives.

Corollary

Don't Stop Dating

Worship together always. There is no stronger bond between a couple than that formed by joint worship. Pray together morning and night, serve together, and attend church together.

Work harder at your marriage than at anything else. It's more important than anything else !

Law Number Seven

Marry Well and Forever

Train up a child in the way he should go;
and when he is old, he will not depart from it.

Proverbs 22:6

The Eighth Law

About fifteen years ago, I used to take the same route to and from work each day. There was one intersection with a stoplight which always seemed to catch me going both ways. As I sat at that stoplight day after day, I watched one of the great tragedies of our time unfold. On one corner was an elderly-care center, where the aged and infirm had been placed. I seldom saw any signs of visitors. More disturbing, however, was the day-care center on the opposite corner. Again and again, I watched as well-dressed men and women drove in the curved driveway, bundled bleary-eyed children into the building, then rushed out and sped off to their workplaces. At six or seven in the evening the same men and women retrieved their children and drove home. I wondered who was raising those children – it certainly wasn't their parents !

Things haven't changed much over the last two decades, either. More and more children are brought up in day-care centers, or by live-in caretakers, or even worse, by themselves. If you want your children to be loved, if you want them to grow up as kind, hard-working, and productive members of society ... raise them yourselves.

You and your spouse must talk about childrearing prior to your marriage. Decide how you want to raise them – together. The need for a mother and a father is as old as the human race. Despite the fact that there are fewer two parent homes these days, those complete nuclear families are the sources of our happiest and most well-balanced people. Watch your own parents and others' parents; observe their techniques and make plans to apply those methods you approve of, and plan to avoid the mistakes they have made.

There are some basic ideas which must be applied in order to do a good job raising your children. I once attended a meeting for Boy Scout leaders. The speaker astounded every listener when he said, "I could take any one of your Scout troops and make every boy in the troop an Eagle Scout !" The audience suddenly grew silent. He continued on, "I could make every boy an Eagle, because I know how much time it takes ... and I'm willing to put in the time." The same thing applies to raising children; it takes time – a lot of time. You have probably heard a good deal about spending quality time with children so that you don't have to spend as much overall time with them. Hogwash. Children need a lot of time. You must spend time with each child individually as well as with the family as a whole. Help them with their projects. Play with them and have fun with them.

Corollary

Take the Time Your Children Need

Children have a multitude of activities they are involved in: school, music, sports, and performances. You name it and they'll have it, and you need to be there with them.

Be at school. The government and the community and the school system are not responsible for your child's education. You are! It is a parental responsibility and cannot be turned over to someone else. Know their teachers, and exercise some input as to who will teach them. Know what they are studying in each subject, and keep up with their studies; make sure they are learning the material. Volunteer in their classrooms and go on their field trips. Join the PTA and help with advisory groups. Know their counselors and the rest of the staff. Attend their programs.

Make sure that each child knows that you love him or her unconditionally. Respect their individuality and their innate talents and gifts. Listen to their problems and concerns – sometimes they just feel like talking, so listen. Show them you love them by supporting them, and just as importantly, tell them that you love them.

Corollary

Show Them and Tell Them You Love Them

Involve your children in family activities as well. Hold a family night every week, and eat dinner together every night. Each child is an important part of the family unit and needs to know that the family cannot function without him or her.

Go to church with your children and teach them to worship. As a family, be of service to others, so your children can feel the joy of service when they are young. Pray together and read the scriptures together.

Teach them to work by working with them. Even little children can learn to do good work and take pride in a job well done.

Have high expectations for your children and they will live up to them. I coached a soccer team of eight year old boys and decided that our primary goal would be to teach them to function as a team. To the dismay of many of the boys' parents, we worked on field position and passing most of the time. But by the end of the season, the boys had grasped the idea that they were much more effective as a team, and their play had risen to a level far above most of the other little teams we played. They had developed an understanding of the team concept which hopefully will stand them in good stead for the rest of their lives. No one thought it possible at the beginning of the season, but high expectations yielded great results.

Corollary

Have High Expectations

Give your children responsibilities commensurate with their abilities and help them fulfill these responsibilities. Make them accountable for their actions and apply the principle of logical consequences when their behavior is less than desirable. Be consistent in your discipline.

Your children are your most important responsibility – don't shortchange them. Study childrearing texts and glean from others valuable techniques and philosophies of parenting. Remember that your children need your time when they are in the first four or five critical years of their lives; they need your time when they are older children, and they need your time when they are preteens and young adults. Invest your time in their future!

Law Number Eight

Raise Your Children Yourself

Only a life lived for others is a life worthwhile.

Albert Einstein

The Ninth Law

There are a multitude of pleasures and joys to be found in life; so many things are fun and give one pleasure. What is the difference between pleasure and joy? Joy is pleasure that is good in the eyes of God. Any number of things may bring us transient pleasure, but joy is lasting and fulfilling.

There are a lot of things that give us pleasure – skiing on a perfect day, receiving a letter from a child, or embracing a loved one. The list of pleasures is endless, and these can help make life a happy existence. But in nearly every instance, the greatest joy can be found when serving our fellow man. When we step outside ourselves to think of and to help others, we experience that greatest of good pleasures.

Our most profound joy is found within the confines of the home and family. But every day we are involved with people who are not in our families, and we may experience that "good" pleasure with them as well.

When I think back to the happiest times for our family, the Christmas season always seems to come to mind. It is a time full of anticipation and happiness, a season of good cheer and fellowship. I remember most vividly that special night each year when we gathered gifts, toys, food, and clothes, boxed everything up, and drove off to make a secret delivery. We carefully drove to our destination and parked in the darkness. You children unloaded the boxes and sneaked up to the front porch of the unsuspecting family. Mom and I sat in the car and watched and laughed as you set the boxes down, then rang the doorbell and ran for cover to make sure we remained anonymous. Never was a family happier than we were after those secret deliveries. The sweet joy of helping others filled the car and sustained us throughout the entire season.

To whom should we be of service? Everyone we come in contact with – and that is a long list of people. Perhaps it would be easier to divide these different people into groups.

We should first and foremost be servants to our families. *Every* aspect of our married life is better if we serve our spouse in every way; think of him or her at every turn. We should help our spouse with his or her work, and with his or her play. We should help our spouse bear his or her burdens, and lighten his or her load. We should serve our children and our extended families. Serving our families expresses and demonstrates the love we have for them.

Our service must extend beyond the bounds of our homes, however. There are a number of ways to serve our fellow man. We should serve in the church and do our very best work there. We can serve elsewhere in the community as well: volunteer at schools, coach teams, serve in local government. There is always someone less privileged than ourselves, and their lives and ours will be benefited by our service.

We can also render service by being involved politically. Vote! Write your representative and express your opinion. Support candidates whose opinions reflect your own. Be involved.

The last point to be made is that occasionally, everyone needs assistance of one kind or another. A helping hand with moving furniture, a meal in times of sickness, a cheerful visit when we are down – whatever it might be, everyone needs help. Even you. Allow others to serve you. Accept their help graciously and thank them. If we don't allow people to serve us, we deny them the blessings and pleasure to be found there. Remember to allow others to help you.

Law Number Nine

Serve and Be Served

How few our real wants,
and how vast our imaginary ones.

Johann Lavater

The Tenth Law

Victor Hugo's <u>Les</u> <u>Miserable</u> begins with a description of Charles Myriel, a humble priest who unexpectedly finds himself a bishop, Monseigneur Bienvenu. As a bishop, he becomes the possessor of all the trappings which go along with that office: the bishop's palace, "a lovely dwelling" with apartments, salons, chambers, a dining hall, a court of honor, arched walkways and a garden lined with magnificent trees. His salary is now 15,000 francs for his personal use and 3,000 francs for carriage expenses. Prior to his appointment, he has had no property and overnight he finds himself a man of some wealth. Next to the bishop's palace there is a small hospital housing twenty-six invalid patients in cramped conditions.

The new bishop's first act is to distribute all but 1000 francs of his allowance to the poor and to call the director of the hospital to the bishop's palace.

" 'Listen, Monsieur Director, to what I have to say. There is evidently a mistake here. There are twenty-six of you in five or six small rooms: there are only three of us, and space for sixty. There is a mistake, I tell you. You have my house and I have yours. Restore mine to me; you are at home.'

The next day the twenty-six poor invalids were installed in the bishop's palace, and the bishop was in the hospital."

This most Christ-like of all literary characters so profoundly influenced Jean Valjean, the novel's main character, that Valjean transformed himself and lived a pure life forever more.

The bishop had a clear view of which things in life he needed for his subsistence, and which things were just wants.

By contrast, I remember a young man, a friend of mine, who sold commercial real estate – and did very well at it. As his business grew, his ego kept pace, and I remember the day he told me, "I need a Mercedes Benz."

"No, you don't; you can't afford one," I replied.

"Yes, I do. I need one."

Not, "I want one," or "I would like one," or "It would really be nice to have one," but "I *need* one." He went ahead and acquired a Mercedes and many of the other trappings of wealth, but in the process, became overextended and eventually lost nearly everything that was near and dear to him.

His was a classic example of "need-want" confusion. We cannot all live like Hugo's Bishop Bienvenu; but we each have to decide which are our "needs" and which are our "wants." There are mental, emotional, spiritual, and physical needs and wants, however this chapter deals with the material needs and wants we all have.

There are basic physical needs which we all share: food, clothing and shelter. We have to have some way of obtaining these things, and we have already discussed work and earning an income which will provide the means to obtain the necessities of life and the amenities we desire. Each of us has to decide about our own needs and wants, and how we will apply our resources.

It's a pretty good idea to differentiate between things we need and things we want early on in life, and to make this determination consistent with our income and savings. It requires a constant review of our own list of needs and wants; which things do we really need, which things do we just want, what must we have, and what would be nice to have.

There are a couple of key points to remember. First, *things* are transitory in nature – they wear out, you tire of them. They are just ... things. Second, wants have a way of pushing reason aside and displacing needs. For example, we all need shelter – an apartment, a house, a trailer, a condominium. The basic need for a warm, dry, clean place to live can be met inexpensively or exorbitantly. I know of a man with a large family who held an excellent, high-paying management position with a large, stable company. He chose to shelter his family in an elegant and expensive home. (There is nothing wrong with expensive houses – if you have met all your basic needs, including educating your children, funding your retirement, providing for emergencies, and paying for the house itself.) Needless to say, his company merged with another and his position was lost. He was out of work for several months and finally had to accept a position which paid substantially less. He was forced to sell his house at a loss, and purchase a smaller, more modest residence. His savings were entirely depleted and he had to borrow money to survive; he is still trying to recover.

Some people have vast economic resources, whether inherited or earned, and can live in mansions and drive expensive automobiles without denting their reserves. Most of us, however, need to balance the need for shelter and transportation with our resources and capabilities. We must have a margin of safety in our purchases, and must remember that material things are just that – things. If you are able at some time to purchase some of your wants, that's great ! Just remember that they are wants and don't purchase them when you still have needs that you haven't paid for. Wants can be material goods – houses, cars, boats, jewelry, clothes, or artwork. They can also be less tangible, like vacations, expensive lessons, or club memberships.

Not too long ago I got the urge to get a new car. My car was perfectly all right; in fact, I liked it very much. I just got this urge. A definite want, not a need. I decided to apply one of my favorite corollaries.

Corollary

If you want something you don't need and really shouldn't get, be patient … the urge will go away.

Now don't get me wrong. I like nice things as well as the next guy, and we all deserve to treat ourselves to nice things or vacations – if we can afford them. Plan for those kinds of things, and buy good quality items, but also plan how to pay for them.

Our society has changed its views of needs and wants over the last fifty years. My Dad took me aside one day when I was about thirty years old and still in the military (we were soon to have our fourth baby). He said, "You can't afford to have all these children. Things are just too expensive these days."

I thought I'd better reply carefully, so I said, "Well, wait a minute. We have a pretty nice house and two cars and we're not spending too extravagantly. What kind of house did you live in when you were thirty?"

He paused and chuckled a little, then said, "We lived in a little, tiny house on Sunnyside Avenue."

"And what kind of car did you drive?"

"We didn't have a car. I rode the streetcar everywhere I went."

We talked for a few moments about the good old days and came to the conclusion that today was probably going to be considered the good old days in thirty or forty years.

That ended our discussion, but it illustrates an important point. Today, couples need two or even three cars. They need a bedroom and bathroom for each child. They need a lake cabin, or a ski boat, or a trip to Hawaii every year ... Need-want confusion.

As your financial situation improves, you can be more flexible with what you purchase, but even those people with great resources must still provide for the basic necessities – both for while they are working and for when they retire. You don't have to be a skinflint but you don't have to be a profligate spender either.

Periodically, it doesn't hurt to review your needs and wants. Sometimes you need to take inventory of your possessions and decide which things are wants, and which are needs, and review what you could do without.

Remember ! Determine which are your needs and which are your wants, and keep them separate. Review them occasionally and keep them in perspective.

Law Number Ten

Beware of
Need-Want Confusion

Debt is a bottomless sea.

Thomas Carlyle

The Eleventh Law

There are a few people who start out in life with enough money to meet their basic needs for as long as they live. It may be that they are less fortunate than the rest of us, because they seldom learn the value of hard work, the importance of struggling, or the satisfaction of economic success. Most of us are not wealthy and we are forced to borrow money to buy very expensive but necessary items.

Historically, we have borrowed money primarily to purchase homes. We ask a bank to lend us a sum of money, and we pay it back over a fifteen or thirty year period. The bank charges us interest on the loan – and they make a lot of money; but at least we get to live in our "own" homes. It is a reasonable way to buy a house. It is not a reasonable way to buy a sofa, or groceries, or a vacation.

These days, borrowing is a lot easier than it used to be – as easy as pulling a card out of your wallet. Borrowing has not been made easier for your convenience; lenders have made borrowing easy, and very expensive, so they can increase their profits. Lenders are not good-hearted and beneficent; they are business people trying to maximize their earnings.

Debt can be a ball and chain you have to drag around with you all your life. Avoid any debt if at all possible !

There are some basic things you should remember if you're considering borrowing money. Do *not* borrow money to pay for something you don't need; remember need-want confusion. Work hard and try to build a nest egg with which you can start yourself on the road to financial independence. (The last law deals with this aspect of financial life.) Try and pay cash for everything you need or want. When you're starting out on your own, you must watch over your resources very carefully. Hopefully, later on in life, you can be less stringent, but you will always have to be attentive to personal finances. A careful budget will help you to do this – if you stick to it. Remember that a budget is a plan and guideline to control expenditures, not a record of spending.

Despite these cautions, there will probably come a time when you have to borrow money. When is that time? There are perhaps only two or three instances which warrant burdening yourself with debt: a home loan, an education loan, or a business loan.

You may be forced to borrow for your education. Advanced education, especially in graduate school, law school, and medical school, has become extremely expensive. Some of the most expensive schools charge outrageous tuitions, and I expect the trend to continue. I remember something my Dad told me about colleges. He spent a year or two recruiting people for a major corporation, and traveled to many of the famous colleges in the nation. He also went to many small, even obscure schools searching for future employees. He said, " Good people can be found at every school, not just the big or expensive ones." A good education can be obtained at any number of institutions. I know that in my graduate school class, the top student had gone to college at a small school in the northern part of the state. Nevertheless, if you have found the place you ought to be, and it requires more money than you have or can earn, then judicious borrowing may be necessary.

Few people can lay down cash for a house these days. The average price for a house is well beyond the reach of most people; so nearly all of us will have to borrow money to purchase our homes. The key is that you must balance your needs and wants with your income and your ability to assume a debt burden. Be reasonable; don't buy more house than you're going to need. A house is not a place to impress others, it is a home for your family to live in.

The last instance where borrowing is sensible is in business. If you have a business requiring a capital investment, you'll probably have to take out a loan. This is in a different category, as it is not a personal loan, but caution is the byword here as well. Businesses can fail, catastrophes can occur; don't borrow more than you need.

Nothing else is so important that you should have to borrow money to pay for it. You should have adequate, life, health, auto, and home insurance so that problems in those areas don't drain your finances and put you into debt.

Automobiles are just that – automobiles. Don't buy a car for which you cannot pay cash. They depreciate, they wear out, they get scratched and dented. It's a huge expense and borrowing to pay for a car is not a justifiable debt. I admit that some of the cars I have owned have looked a little disreputable, but I did own each of them outright. The same thing holds true for vacations, furniture, and other things. Pay cash ! If you can't afford it, don't get it, and most emphatically, don't borrow money to purchase it.

Corollary

Pay cash … If you can't afford it, don't get it !

Credit cards are dangerous. It is so easy to get one and use one that many people get into terrible trouble with them. I would recommend avoiding them altogether if possible, although many businesses require a credit card as a form of identification. Use them sparingly and carefully.

Debt can be a bottomless pit that holds you bound for your entire life. Avoid it !

Law Number Eleven

Steer Clear of Debt

When prosperity comes, don't use all of it.

Confucius

The Twelfth Law

Not long ago I spoke with professional man who has always earned a good income and always will. He told me he had had a lot of fun in his life, had enjoyed many different interests, and had given his family many unique opportunities. We started talking about retirement, and what we would be able to do with the time we would have then. He said, "Oh, I'll never be able to retire."

"What do you mean? " I asked.

He replied, "I haven't saved any money; I'm sure I'll have to work until I die."

Everyone has his or her own dream of financial security. Some people won't be satisfied until they are living on a yacht in the Mediterranean, but most will be satisfied with a great deal less. Generally speaking, however, all of us hope to someday become financially independent. Wouldn't it be wonderful to work hard, save and invest wisely, and then someday be able to retire and live the lifestyle you have chosen – without having to worry about how you're going to pay for your next meal?

It is not an easy goal to reach, but it is

attainable, and hopefully this chapter will give you some ideas to help you on your way.

First and foremost, you and your spouse must establish a budget with respect to your income and stick to it. You cannot function like the government and spend more than you earn – you must live within your means.

Corollary

Spend Less Than You Earn !

It is much easier to follow this corollary if you make a great deal of money, but it applies to *everyone*. I read the biography of a man who ran a major corporation in the United States, and remember him stating that he just couldn't live on less than $900,000 a year ! Most of us can get along on a lot less. There are some basic expenditures that will not go away. Taxes, insurance, mortgages, food bills, donations, etc. all must be paid regularly. But each month, after you have paid for all these things, pay yourself. This doesn't mean you take some money each month and blow it on something you don't need. It means you should take ten percent of your gross pay and sock it away. You'll need to have enough money for a down payment on a house or to begin your retirement savings. Put this savings plan in your budget and adhere to it.

Corollary

Pay Yourself

When you are about to purchase a house, there are some thoughts you should consider. Again, buy a reasonable home – if you're just starting out, buy a starter home. Shop around for the best loan you can find from several reliable lending institutions.

In Chapter Two I mentioned the personal living session at a professional meeting we attended. One of the speakers discussed personal finances and lifestyles. He said that he had made and lost several fortunes in his lifetime, and that he had some advice to give us concerning financial security. He paused and with great conviction said, "The best advice I can give you is to buy a reasonable home and pay off your mortgage."

I agree. The best savings program is to pay your mortgage off early and actually *own* your own home. When you own your home, it is a haven of safety and security – no one can take it away from you. Additionally, the burden of mortgage payments is lifted, and this money can be applied to retirement savings.

Few people live in the same house their whole lives; you may be transferred to another city, your family may outgrow your house, or you may simply want to trade up. My Dad gave me some good advice about home ownership. He said, " Treat every house as if it will be the home you live in forever."

It's good advice. Your house becomes your home. You'll care for it, improve it, enhance it, and beautify it. If you end up leaving it, it will be worth more to you in every way than it was when you bought it.

Corollary

Treat every home like you'll never leave it.

Even the best-laid plans sometimes go awry. Illness, war, natural disaster, business failure, economic collapse, and who knows what else – all these things can strike anyone. Be prepared for such an emergency. It may seem quite impractical to most people, but keeping a year's supply is an excellent idea. A year's supply of what? You should have a year's supply of money, food, clothing, and fuel if possible. I know people who have lived off their year's supply of food while weathering a financial crisis.

Corollary

Keep a Year's Supply

Sometime or other, you must think about your retirement. Thinking about it earlier is better than thinking about it later; those who wait until later often wait until it is too late. There are some general principles to remember.

Rely on *yourself* to fund your retirement ! Don't rely on the government.

It's a good bet that Social Security will be "insecure" by the time your turn comes around. Don't count on an inheritance, either. That would be nice, and every parent would like to leave something to the children, but you can never predict what might happen. The company you work for might have a great retirement program, but companies fail, and retirement funds are lost. Set realistic goals for accruing your own retirement fund and work to meet them.

I should probably comment on investing your savings, although I am certainly no expert on this aspect of financial planning. You should probably invest conservatively and plan for the long haul. Get rich quick schemes don't work, lotteries are always won by someone else, and speculation is usually a road map to financial loss. Be conservative. You'll have to work hard for your money; don't gamble it away.

Corollary

If it sounds too good to be true …
it is.

Where should you invest your money? I don't know. I don't think anyone really does. There are a lot of people who are willing to invest your money for you and accept payment for their services. I would listen to several conservative experts and then invest cautiously. As a general rule, invest in large, sound, fairly conservative companies that are well run. Invest in companies whose products *you* personally like and *you* personally use. Invest your money in good companies you know, like, and trust.

Have a plan to earn money, a plan to spend money, but also a plan to save money.

Law Number Twelve

Save up a Storm

Well, there you have it. Twelve laws for happy living. There is nothing too fancy about them; most everything in this little book you've been told already, and the rest is pretty much just common sense. But it doesn't hurt to have it written down. Mom and I want you to be successful, well adjusted, and most importantly ... happy.

I love you,

Dad